I Want It All

Troy McClain, Jr.

INTRODUCTION

In this book I do not claim to be all-knowing in avoiding the many problems of life that we all face. Problems and circumstances are inevitable and unavoidable. I do, however, believe that the challenges we encounter are merely disguises for opportunities waiting to be seized. In the following pages I share with you tools and experiences that have helped me hone in on who I am and most importantly who I am becoming. It is my prayer that after you have completed this book that you will become weary of mediocrity and never settle for anything less than all of what God has in store for you!

"Beloved, I wish above all things that thou mayest prosper and be in health, even as thy soul prospereth"
3 John V.2

I WANT IT ALL

TABLE OF CONTENTS

I WANT IT ALL

ACKNOWLEDGMENTS

First, I would like to thank my Lord and Savior Jesus Christ, as without Him this book would not be possible. I would also like to thank and acknowledge my parents Kathleen and Troy McClain, Sr., my Pastor Antonio and 1st Lady Catherine Gathers, my grandparents Reverend Dr. Edward McClain, Jr., Sarah McClain and my dear friend Cynthia Beaulieu.

Had it not been for their unwavering support and prayers, this book would not have come to fruition. I thank, love and appreciate you all from the bottom of my heart.

1
THE POWER OF A SEED

Every seed planted has the potential to grow and what grows depends on what is being fed.

I believe that every seed starts as a thought. It is said that humans have anywhere from 12,000-60,000 thoughts per day. Thoughts are juggled between our own and/or those that have been sown into us by others, but how they are created is irrelevant. Whether they are developed and produced is up to us. Studies have shown that every negative thought demands at least 17 good thoughts to overtake that of the bad, which means we possess the power not to germinate those thoughts into anything grandiose.

In Chapter 1 of *Uncover Your Potential*" by Dr. Myles Munroe, he discloses a powerful principle about the importance of a seed, recognizing it as the most potent element in nature. He suggests that if you are holding a seed in your hand and someone asks you, "What is in your hand?" you would undoubtedly respond, "a seed" without acknowledging the seed's nature. Your answer would be fact but not truth because the seed may be a seed in your hand, but it holds the potential to produce a forest.

When a farmer plants seeds in the ground he also makes a commitment to nurture and protect them with the expectation that in the future they will produce a crop. Depending on the species of the crop the soil's condition should be a temperature of about 55-60 degrees Fahrenheit. The seeds should be no more than one inch deep and approximately four to six inches apart. Once planted, he then monitors the field for any trespassers or anything that could stunt the seeds' growth or annihilate their existence.

As a young boy growing up, I struggled mightily in school. It was not uncommon to hear nasty words like, "dummy," "stupid," or "retard." Those were all forms of negative seeds that could have become a reality if I had allowed them to take root. I fortunately had the right kind of people around me that would not allow me to be infected, but we'll discuss that in a later chapter.

You must understand and know that God has intentionally blessed each and every one of us with ideas (seeds) to bear fruit. It is up to us to defend and guard those ideas from all possible threats. God may have given you the idea to start a business, non-profit organization, invention or write a book. Whatever it is it was conceived in your mind to produce something. The very moment it appears, there will be doubters, skeptics, or haters, some of which are the closest people to you. But just as the farmer secures his crops from insects, weeds or anything hazardous to the seeds, you must defend your ideas and only focus on their manifestation.

"Whatever you focus on the longest becomes the strongest"
~ Les Brown

"As a man thinketh in his heart so is he."
Proverbs 23:7

In retrospect our thoughts, whether positive or negative become who we are because of repetition. Every day you feed that idea, dream or goal the more it becomes a reality. Steve Harvey said, "If you see it in your mind, you can hold it in your hand. It all starts with what you're willing to believe..." I believe that you will succeed, do you?

Say this prayer with me:

Dear Lord, thank you for entrusting me with multiple ideas. Continue to guide and cover my thought process. Help me to accept what is good, reject what is not and fulfill them all . In your name I pray.

Amen

2
IT STARTS WITH YOU

"The man who says he can, and the man who says he cannot, are both correct."
Confucius

Every day begins and ends with you. The middle, however, is where most of us face our greatest fears, challenges and opposition, which I believe, is people. Everyone longs for a sense of acceptance and validation; in other words, for people to affirm their ambitions. So if in fact, they're deflected or disapproved we're less likely to pursue them. The dilemma, however, is that we could forfeit a business, a house, a position or even an opportunity all because someone wouldn't endorse what God gave you.

They say that most people who deter others from ambitions and outlandish goals are unable to perform them themselves. People only tend to support what they can envision themselves doing. But what happens when the "you" God made you, collides with the "you" people perceive you to be? Do you prolong what God said to do now? Do you get a second opinion? Or perhaps you just wait until the majority can SEE what God showed you?

The Miami Mass Choir used to sing a song entitled, "It is For Me". The point of the song I believe is to underline that what God has for you, simply put, is for you. You can't expect anyone else to co·sign what was meant to be owned by you individually. It has to start with you believing what God said, believing it will manifest and then believing beyond the naysayers.

Before Michael Jordan became the six· time NBA champion global icon, he was a high school student cut from the Varsity basketball team. His coach stated that he wasn't good enough and should contribute his skills to other sports. Rather than adhering to the coach's words he convinced himself that next year would be his year. The rest as they say is history; he not only came back the next year and performed exceptionally well in high school but he excelled throughout college as well as the NBA. He rightfully earned the title, "Greatest of all time". He made a self-defining choice to rise above the noise to become what he became. The true testament of what you believe you can do is not when everyone says yes, but when nothing or no one suggests that you're the one to do it.

Every person of wealth and success had to overcome resistance and negativity at some point. From Genesis to Revelation cross-pollinating to Thomas Edison with the light bulb or Barack Obama being the first African-American President, it's a conscious decision that must begin with you, forthrightly believing in you. Once you convince yourself that you can you will become unconquerable and nothing will be beyond your reach.

If you don't believe in yourself you indirectly authorize others to GPS what you should do with your life. Les Brown said, "Someone's opinion of you does not have to become your reality." Your reality is what you think of yourself. IT starts with YOU!

"I will praise thee; for I am fearfully and wonderfully made: marvelous are thy works; and that my soul knoweth right well." **Psalm: 139:14**

Say this Prayer with me:

Dear Lord, Help me to see myself as you see

me. Rebuild my confidence, my self-esteem and reconnect me to the dreams you've given me. And make sure I fulfill all you've assigned to my name. In your name I Pray.

Amen

3
YOUR CONNECTION IS YOUR PROTECTION

Your net-worth is your network

When I was a youngster I would occasionally hear, "Birds of a feather flock together", or "You are the company you keep." As a child those words had no significance or value. At that time they were simply just phrases commonly uttered out of the mouth of those superior to me. As I grew older I began to understand that those same words spoke volumes to me in school, church and in life.

I believe that the greatest power of influence comes from the people you call your friends. Unbeknownst to you they help steer what you wear, whom you date, and where you go in life. As absurd as this may sound ask yourself this question, "How many times have you been in a situation when a decision had to be made and you needed a second opinion?" If you paused or smiled then you too have given someone the authority to influence what you should do, but is that a good or bad thing? That solely depends on whom you have in your "circle of friends". If you find yourself always unmotivated, disconnected and stuck, then it's time to do a self-analysis of yourself to find out what needs to be changed.

Dr. Van Moody wrote a book entitled "The People Factor". The subtitle of the book underscores how building great relationships and ending bad ones unlock your God-given purpose. He believes as I do that relationships are vital, yet sometimes they can be detrimental to the destination of where we end up. The question is what does that mean? Most friendships and relationships consist of people who have similar interests as you do or who care about the same things. The problem that confuses most people is that what's good *to* them, may not be good *for* them. Unfortunately, they never reach the height of their potential because their surroundings never demanded it.

In Chapter 5 of his book, "The People Factor," Dr. Moody subtitles the chapter, "The Law of Selectivity", which basically means you can't be friends with everyone. If the people around you don't challenge or provoke you to do better, then perhaps it's time to change your crew. It seems as though that is a harsh thing to say but you've got to protect what God gave you. Eagles fly with eagles and chickens run with chickens.

Dr. Moody puts it this way. "Relationships are like elevators, the right ones take you up, the wrong ones take you down." To add to that I say the good ones will keep you stuck. There's nothing like having friends that are all going in the same direction. .

The Bible says in Proverbs 18:24, "*A man that hath friends must shew himself friendly: and there is a friend that sticketh closer than a brother.*" Being as though they are closer to you than your family, it best suits you to choose them wisely and for the benefit of where you are going because after all, your connection is your protection!

"He who walks with the wise grows wise, but a companion of fools suffers harm."
Proverbs 13:20

Say this prayer with me:

Lord, help me be connected to people that only push me to greatness, The courage to disconnect from those who don't, And to be watchful for attachments. In Your name I Pray. AMEN!

4
YOUR PURPOSE

The two most important days in your life are the day you are born and the day you find out why
Mark Twain.

I believe that most people go through their entire life dazed and confused as to what their purpose is. The haunting question that constantly resides in our minds is what is my purpose? Beyond marriage, kids, good job, possessions why are we here? While watching Steve Harvey's "Last Standup Comedy" he said someone tweeted him, "Your career is what you're paid for, and your calling is what you're made for." God has assigned a specific purpose for each of us to fulfill and until we are operating in it, our lives will remain unfulfilled.

The world paints a picture that recognizes money, houses, cars and fame as confirmation that we are successful and we must be living in our purpose when in reality millions of wealthy people that possess countless material things still feel empty. Webster defines the word "purpose" as the reason for which something is done or created for or for which something exists. Your purpose is not what you own, where you work, or even what your profession is.

It's the feeling that liberates you beyond riches and fame or anyone knowing your name. No one can tell you your purpose except GOD. People may know what you're good at, but not what you are good for.

Your purpose is an internal contentment regardless of affirmation or validation from anyone because you feel complete while doing it. There isn't any amount of money that will satisfy you of that thirst or longing for it or a house big enough to occupy, or a person smart enough to tell you what you should be doing. It's got to resonate within you no matter how big or small. Once you own and harness it, your life will feel ALIVE! Mother Teresa's purpose was to travel the world as a Missionary. Martin Luther King, Jr.'s purpose was to stand up for all people to receive equal rights. Most people sojourn throughout life only surviving without ever really knowing what it feels like to LIVE.... I challenge you to live on purpose in your purpose!

In life we've all been awarded a chance to make a name or make a difference. As for me I choose the latter.

"But for this very purpose have I let you live, that I might show you my power, and that my name may be declared throughout all the earth." **Exodus 9:16**

Say this prayer with me:

Lord, divorce me from my fears. Marry me to my Destiny. So I can birth my Purpose. In your name I Pray. AMEN

5
THE PLAN

You were born to win, but to be a winner,

you must plan to win, prepare to win, and

expect to win.

Zig Ziglar

It's one thing to know your purpose
and another to have a plan. The
Bible says that we ought to write
the vision and make it plain (Habakkuk

2:2). Helen Keller put it this way. *"It's a terrible thing to see and have no vision."* It's almost as if we know where we want to end up but have no execution plan to get there. It's as if it's just going to fall in your lap because it's your purpose. Sorry to be the one to tell you but that's not the way it works. Once you've found your purpose write down your plan as to how you will make it happen.

In the movie *Pursuit of Happyness*, Will Smith played a character by the name of Chris Gardner, a struggling salesman who came across a stock broker and made a conscious decision at that moment to work on Wall Street. It took him a few seconds to determine what he wanted to do but much longer to get there. Despite the difficulties he faced he remained committed to the plan regardless of the process.

In their song "Can't Give Up Now" Mary Mary says, "I just can't give up now, I've come too far from where I started from. Nobody told me the road would be easy and I don't believe He brought me this far to leave me." When God gives us something to manifest or bring-forth it's not going to be easy but He assures us that since He gave it to you He'll never leave you. So stick with the plan!

I know you may be thinking as I did. This sounds encouraging and moving but things NEVER go as planned! If that's what you're thinking then you would be absolutely correct. When all else fails, the trail seems dismal and the skies grow cloudy, it's in that moment when God

27

intervenes and says, "It's all going according to my plan." The Prophet Isaiah warrants our attention in the fifty-fifth chapter of his book and the eighth verse which says, "For *my thoughts are not your thoughts, neither are your ways my ways, saith the LORD.*" What appears to be unchartered and off course, plays a much larger part than what we ever imagined.

When God implores you to write out your plan it's not because the plan will work the way you wrote it but because despite the degree of difficulty and opposition you know you'll face, you believe in what He said; so write it out anyway!

There is something that's brewing within you that came into your mind or resonated within your spirit that seems outlandish, idiotic, and illogical. The moment you take it from your mind and put it on a piece of paper you've told God, "I believe." You may not know how, what or when it will happen but the assurance to God is that you wrote it out and began moving towards it. It is a cry to heaven saying, "Okay, God, it's your turn." It's important to note that after traveling at comfortable speeds while working the plan you will face adversity and detours, but despite it all stick with the plan because it's all working accordingly to His plan, and in the end you will prevail!

'For I know the plans I have for you,'
says the Lord, 'plans for well-being and not
for trouble, to give you a future and a hope."
Jeremiah 29:11

Say this prayer with me:

Lord, Order my Steps. Instruct my Ways. Keep me in your Path. That I would follow your plan for my life. In Your Name I Pray.

Amen.

6
THE PAST

You are not your past but a product from it if you choose to be.

After you have found your purpose and have written out your plan everything else is smooth sailing, right? Unfortunately, no. The reality is that the precise moment you make a life-changing decision, in that same instance your deepest wounds become visible again and you've traveled back in time to the harrowing experience that you never got over.

As I mentioned in Chapter One, I struggled immensely throughout my middle and high school years. Although I had gotten through it, it was not through with me. As I grew older and began to delve into the world through jobs and other opportunities I found myself limiting my abilities based on words from my past that I never fully erased or faced. So anytime I faced opportunities disguised as obstacles I would settle for "good enough" when God wanted me to have it all. I hid behind those comments that were made to me as a child to allow me as Pastor Jamal H. Bryant says, to be, "Victimized by POOR. That's passing over opportunities repeatedly." In his book, Bishop Rudolph Mckissick, Jr. says, "You can't fix what you won't face." If you're unwilling to face your past it will always paralyze you from ever reaching the promise God has for you.

Ask yourself, how many times have you passed up a promotion, job opportunity, moving, or a business? The list goes on and on all because you failed to deal with that thing or that person; it affects your present and impacts your future until you face it. It may sometimes dwindle, fade or even change forms but it doesn't dissipate completely until you stand flat footed and refuse to surrender to it or them.

In 2004 Jamie Foxx starred in the movie called "Ray" where he played Ray Charles.

As you may know Ray Charles was an excellent musician with an unimpressionable irreplaceable voice that shook the world of music. Throughout the movie despite his success musically and financially Ray had a problem that ultimately almost got the best of him. Ray started taking heroin consistently, which could have cost him his life or his career. He was eventually admitted to a rehab facility and underwent being completely liberated from the addiction of heroin. When Ray was a child he witnessed his brother drown in a tub of water and allowed himself to bear the blame for most of his life. Every time he saw an image of his brother in his mind he used heroin to avoid having to discuss or deal with it. Ray's way out was heroin, but what's yours? Is it fear, doubt, failure, words, or unforgiveness?

Whatever it is you've got to overcome it and face it because greater awaits you on the other side. The devil uses your past against you because he knows if you can ever get over it or them you're destined to excel and exceed. Don't allow another day to go by without handling the affairs of your past because your future awaits you!

"Brethren, I count not myself to have apprehended: but this one thing I do, forgetting those things which are behind, and reaching forth unto those things which are before." **Philippians 3:13**

Say this prayer with me:

Dear Lord help me to confront and deal with my past. Cherish and take full advantage of the present. And be ready for what the future has in store for me. In Your Name I pray. Amen

7

THE PROMISE

God never made a promise that was too

good to be true

Dwight Moody

The dictionary defines the word promise as a declaration or assurance that one will do a particular thing or that a particular thing will happen. In this definition the word that stands out to me the most is the word "will". It simply states that a promise cannot be solidified without the words, I will.

As a child I remember the times that my parents said, "If you do this, I promise you will get that." The message that they were conveying to me was, I guarantee that if you do exactly as I tell you what to do, you will then reap the benefits of your obedience.

Just as we receive the benefits of obedience from our natural parents, our heavenly father assures us that we will receive the blessings of His promises if we obey His Word. Isaiah 1:19 says, "If you are willing and obedient, you will eat the good of the land." Whenever God commits to doing something in His word rest assured, it will happen.

I recently taught a Bible study entitled "All I need is His Word". We talked about several biblical characters including Abraham, Job, and Joseph, who received a word from God and every time the promise was delayed there was a process that needed to take place. Once the process was completed the promise was manifested, but it took time and because of their faith and obedience the Word of God came to pass. No matter how preposterous or absurd it may seem God's word is sure. The biggest dilemma for most believers is that they are more concerned with the HOW it will be done, rather than just believing WHO said it.

When God promises us something and

speaks a word to us, it is usually unfavorable pertaining to where we are in life. Nothing about where we are remotely suggests that what we hear is possible. For example, while working at a fast food restaurant or as a bus driver, God may whisper in your ear that you are going to be a multi-millionaire in business. It doesn't seem possible based on the current circumstances so instead of continuing to reach forth you settle for only the visible, believable and obtainable.

There is a lot we can learn from a child's perspective. Children operate with a sense of fearlessness, submission and obedience with no worries that they will receive the candy, money or play time. The difference between them and adults is the ability to reason. In other words, when a child hears their parents promise them something, all they hear is Mommy and Daddy are going to make it happen if we do this. They haven't reached the age to refute or concern themselves with how Mommy and Daddy are going to pull it off. All they hear is who said it. The rest of it doesn't matter.

I'm sure you've heard the phrase "delayed doesn't mean denied" and most of the time God is delaying the manifestation of His word because we are either not ready for it or we haven't started moving towards what was promised. Dr. Martin Luther King, Jr. said, "Faith is taking the first step even when you don't see the whole staircase." Regardless of the proclamation you must be willing to move towards it to get it even though along the way there will be moments of uncertainty, darkness and even pain. Whatever circumstances come or whatever happens you keep going until what God said matches what you SEE.

Langston Hughes said in his poem, *Mother to Son,* "Now son I'll tell you life for me ain't been no crystal stair but I'se still climbing." When God is in the picture spend no time worrying about it -- just believe it. I'm learning that all of what God has pronounced over my life is already etched and completed. I just have to be willing to survive the journey before reaching the destination.

Has God promised you something years ago, expansion, increase, or franchise but because of where you are in life today you wrote it off? I want to challenge and compel you to believe what was said and not what you don't have.   Don't lose your promise behind doubts, fear or what is invisible. For God always, and I repeat always, comes through with a promise!

"God is not a man, that he should lie; neither the son of man, that he should repent: hath he said, and shall he not do it? Or hath he spoken, and shall he not make it good?" **Numbers 23:19**

Say this prayer with me:

Dear Lord teach me to trust what you have promised.   When what you said doesn't match   what   I   see.   Teach   me   to continuously believe. In your name I pray. AMEN

I WANT IT ALL

.

8

HAVE FAITH

"If you want something you've never had,
you must be willing to do something you've
never done before."

Thomas Jefferson

I believe the most commonly used
scripture for faith is found in the
book of Hebrews 11:1 which says,
"Now faith is the substance of things hoped

for, the evidence of things not seen". The question is what does this mean in practical terms and how can we apply this principle to our lives? I'm under the persuasion that the overwhelming majority of people know how to define faith but fail to apply it. So what is it then? Faith is the assurance of belief knowing that whatever goal you have, will be attained despite any interference against your desired target. It is to move forward with expectancy that the target will be reached no matter what you face.

Every person reading this book has aspirations, dreams, goals or something that God told them they would accomplish without giving them the details. Simply put, God expects total cooperation without explanation. And that my friend, is where faith comes in. To make matters more problematic God usually tells you these things when nothing around you suggests that it is possible.

Bishop Rudolph McKissick, Jr. put it this way. "There is a promise and then there is a process. We can't get to the promise without going through the process of our faith being tested and challenged." He also says that the promise is in God's hands and the process is in our hands. The devil shows up in the process hoping to deter us from believing that it is possible to accomplish our goals.

The Bible speaks of a man called, "The Father of Faith" better known as Abraham. God commanded Abraham and his family and told them to leave everything they had behind and go to a place that God would show them. I know you're thinking, huh? God didn't even tell Abraham where he was going, He just said, "Leave!" What most fail to acknowledge or realize is that Abraham was already wealthy with land and livestock. God asked him to leave everything and rely on faith in God to lead him.

I believe the greatest thing that God has for us can only be obtained by activating our faith. Most people rely on logic but logic defies the concept of faith. Basically everything we do is only because it logically makes sense. But the moment it doesn't make sense we tend to gather millions of excuses as to why we shouldn't do it. Don't miss your blessed place because you don't know HOW or WHEN it is going to get done. I've learned throughout my life that God works in the element of the unknown when there is no evidence that suggests we are close or we are going to make it... my friends that is faith. In an interview once when someone asked Steve Harvey how to become successful, he replied, "You have to jump!" There is no way around it. Every successful person had to jump to get where they are. The question is, are you willing to jump? Are you willing to defy the law of logic, statistics and opinionated people? Will you close this chapter and write your book, start your business plan, apply for the house, or make a move to another state? To jump you have to have faith that God won't allow you to fall. You will get challenged, bumped, and maybe even bruised but when you jump you release God to work. On your mark, get set, JUMP!

"But when you ask, you must believe and not doubt, because the one who doubts is like a wave of the sea, blown and tossed by the wind." **James 1:6**

Say this Prayer with me:

Dear Lord deflate my doubt. Inflate my FAITH. Help me trust and believe always. That anything I set out to do I will do it. In Jesus' Name

9
I FAILED

"I haven't failed, I just found 10,000 ways
that won't work"
Thomas Edison

Ladies and gentlemen I believe thoroughly that no one can be successful without failing. It is the most powerful and undervalued principle towards success. Every highly successful person on the planet has failed in route to fulfilment. The difference between failing and failure is those who STOP. There is a picture that I see often on social media of a man swinging a pick trying to reach diamonds and as he gets within one swing he does the unthinkable; he quits. He figures it is futile to swing anymore because it won't ever amount to anything. In that moment he puts the pick down, turns around and becomes a failure.

How many times have you kept the faith and the momentum laced with drive and still no visible proof that you were close to or going to succeed? If you're like most, then your answer would be, "thousands of times".

Realistically after you've found your

niche, developed it and matured it, that doesn't mean it will take flight immediately. It will take time, persistence and most importantly patience. Look at it like this. The finish line is your desired target or goal. In order to get there you have to run the full course of the race. There will be moments of weariness, exhaustion, aggravation and doubt. But no matter what you do, don't quit and don't stop running. It's not about your speed or your strength but it's about your endurance. You must possess the WILL to press and continue against all odds, and never acquiesce to failure.

I read in a book somewhere that the founder of KFC, Colonel Sanders, wasn't born wealthy or even went to a prestigious college and he never had a promising career in a trade. All he had was a recipe, his car and a white suit. At the age of 65 he took his recipe and traveled around searching for a restaurant or business that would entertain his innovative idea. Colonel Sanders came across 1,009 no's before somebody finally said yes. What makes his story so remarkable is not his success but his resilience to unwillingly embrace failure.

The price for greatness requires down payments of suffering, pain, agony and yes, failing. I'm under the persuasion that the reward for continued failing is guaranteed success! I have a question for you. When you get told "No" (because you will), will you stop? When you get denied (because you will), will you stop? When you get tired, lonely, weary, and discouraged (because you will), will you quit? The answer ought to be no! God never said reaching the best place would be easy, but it is most definitely worth it. Vashawn Mitchell in his song says, "Sooner or later it'll turn in your favor." Don't quit! Turn failing into success!

"But I have prayed for thee, that thy faith fail not: and when thou art converted, strengthen thy brethren." **Luke 22:32**

Say this Prayer With Me:

Dear Lord, give me the courage. To continue, the strength. To hold on, and the endurance to keep going and never quit! In Your Name I pray. Amen.

I WANT IT ALL

10
BROKEN

Sometimes you have to be broken in

order to be made.

T.D Jakes

Recently I stumbled across a YouTube video that captivated my attention and had fully consumed me by the end the video. It was Oprah Winfrey doing a segment on Bishop

T. D Jakes in a new series called the "Next Chapter with Oprah". She attended his Sunday morning service and had a one-on-one interview with him afterwards. During his sermon he uttered, "Sometimes you have to be broken in order to be made." Immediately I shouted at the computer, "That's good, Bishop!"

In context that doesn't make sense, right? Or does it... He went on to say that every single person he knows that is massively successful, has undergone succumbing to the unfortunate truth of being broken. In other words you must endure pain before being able to understand and appreciate pleasure. I know that is not something we like to hear or digest but truthfully once I understood the purpose behind it, it became easier to accept. God in His infinite wisdom prepares us with brokenness before being elevated. There is something in pain that equips us for where we are going. Look at it like this.

Pretend you are walking up stairs that lead to your desired dream or goal at the top but as you are walking up, you step on nails, tacks, maybe you even break a toe; all unwanted I'm sure. But what you didn't know was that at the top there are bigger nails, longer tacks and bigger holes waiting for you to step on or fall in. Because you experienced pain and injuries on your expedition you developed acumen to avoid pitfalls and setbacks in your destined place. God allows things to happen to cultivate humility and maturity so that when you get to your targeted destination you will be able to stay there. Steve Harvey, Tyler Perry and Oprah Winfrey have all been victimized by some form of brokenness but even through their hellacious trials and tribulations, they have still managed to breakthrough and all are now made.

Don't allow moments of irritation to cause you to make a permanent decision to forfeit ever reaching your manifestation. If you are in the middle of something hurtful or painful, understand that it is just a pit stop.

It isn't over until what God professed over your life matches where you are in reality. Standby because you're just being made!

"When Jesus saw him lie, and knew that he

had been now a long time in that case, he saith unto him, Wilt thou be made whole?"
John 5:6

Say this Prayer with Me:

Dear Lord, strengthen me while being broken. Push me when I want to give up. Mature me so when I'm made I'll stay there. In your name. Amen.

11

THERE IS MUCH MORE IN YOU

"Never settle for good when abundance lurks around the corner"

The Bible says in John 10:10, "The thief cometh not, but for to steal, and to kill, and to destroy: I am come that they might have life, and that they might have it more abundantly." In a practical sense the devil or the enemy desires nothing more than for us to settle for good throughout life when we were born for abundance. He aspires to steal our dreams, kill our faith and destroy any inkling of hope that there is in us. Good is much better than bad or average but what if there is something even better?

What if there is something more that awaits you? The only way to get it would be to leave the good, to sojourn to a place you've never been to achieve something greater. Does the name Oprah Winfrey ring a bell? Oprah was a radio personality, news anchor, actress, TV talk show host, and now has her own network entitled OWN, Oprah Winfrey Network. Oprah transcended every area she ventured into, becoming America's 1st black woman billionaire. The clouding question is how did she do this? Simply put, she did not allow her success in one area to limit or disengage her from traversing to fully expanding all of what she was given to produce. Most of us meander through our lives until we find that the thing that we're good at causes us to settle and never explore the endless possibilities beyond what was good. The danger of doing well is thinking that it's the destination and not just a part of the journey.

In his book, "Act Like a Success Think Like a Success" chapter 13 which is entitled, "Never be afraid to reinvent yourself", Steve Harvey expresses his willingness to allow his gift to create new opportunities that he fearlessly walked into. He is widely known across the globe as a comedian who cross-pollinated into the Gospel stage as well. Steve went from being a comedian, to hosting Apollo, to his own sitcom, to a radio show, writing a book, hosting "Family Feud" to now having his own Steve Harvey Show. He attributes all of his accomplishments to always being open to what's next. I think we have brought injustice to the word "success" in totality. Success is not a destination.

Success is not achievements and accomplishments in one area. Success is rather forthrightly expanding our gift to multiple facets until the day we die. It's a journey. Most people dwell in what is, rather than what could be.

There are millions of people across the

world in addition to Oprah Winfrey and Steve Harvey who understand the truth of limitless success. The question is what will you do beyond what you've already done? Will you make your Salon a Spa? Will you expand your business or open multiple locations? Or will you just be content with good and leave the greater locked in you?

I don't believe you're reading this book by happenstance or coincidence. I believe this was God ordained just to remind you that God has more in store for you than what you could ever imagine.... As of this moment tell good enough, "Bye Bye" because you're headed towards your abundance.

"Ye are of God, little children, and have overcome them: because greater is he that

is in you, than he that is in the world."

1 John 4:4

Say this prayer with me

Dear Lord, help me to never settle for good. Be content with great. And willingly ready to move to acquire my abundance. In Jesus' Name. Amen.

12
THE DASH

Life is not about your duration but about your donation

I n the first chapter of this book I mentioned one of my favorite teachers, world renowned author, Dr. Myles Munroe. Little did I know that shortly after starting this book that he would transition home to be with the Lord.

I dedicate this chapter solely to him and the principles he stood for.

When you think of the term "dash" what do you think of? Running, sprinting? Those are true but in this instance its meaning is severely different. When looking at a tombstone, other than the person's name you see the year they were born and the year they died. The dash is the symbol in between the day they arrived and the day they died. Our lives are not about how long we live but about what we contributed while we were here. I know that sounds eerie and gloomy but it's the truth. The dash on our tombstone is the most important part about our lives because it represents what we did with the time that we've been allotted. I've heard dozens of sermons and even purchased several of Dr. Monroe's books and what he talked about more than anything was leadership, purpose, potential and contribution.

In one of his sermons he stated that he had prewritten out his obituary and would look at it as a constant reminder that his time was limited. He said that the richest place in the world wasn't on Wall Street, banks, gold mines or off-shore accounts. He said the richest place in the world is in the cemetery because millions of people have died with unfulfilled purposes, robbing the world of what was assigned to their life. The dash is an opportunity to grasp life and live it to the fullest. Your life is not about your duration, but about your donation.

God has rewarded each and every one of

us with unique gifts and ideas and aspirations that have only been given to us to contribute to the world. It is my prayer that you fulfil every single idea or goal that God has tailored for you to produce. The depth of this chapter is not to focus on death or dying though that is inevitable, but to fully take advantage of the dash so that when your time comes the focus won't be about when you died but what you did when you were alive.

Time is the most valuable commodity that most of us waste and wish we had more of. Your dreams, goals, aspirations...I encourage you to start them NOW! It may not happen overnight, but with prayer, persistence and patience the promise will come to pass. It's not only your time but your turn, in the words of Dr. Myles

Munroe, "Live full and die empty!"

The greatest tragedy in life is not death
but a life without a purpose
Dr. Myles Munroe

Say This Prayer With Me:

Dear Lord, help me not to leave this earth.
Without doing all you've pronounced over
my life. In your name. Amen

50613718R00046

Made in the USA
Charleston, SC
03 January 2016